Telling the Truth

For a free color catalog describing Gareth Stevens' list of high-quality books and multimedia programs, call 1-800-542-2595 (USA) or 1-800-461-9120 (Canada). Gareth Stevens Publishing's Fax: (414) 225-0377.
See our catalog, too, on the World Wide Web: http://gsinc.com

The author and original publisher would like to thank the staff and pupils of the following schools for their help in the making of this book: St. Barnabas Church of England Primary School, Pimlico; Kenmont Primary School, Hammersmith & Fulham; St. Vincent de Paul Roman Catholic School, Westminster; Mayfield Primary School, Cambridge; St. Peter's Church of England Primary School, Sible Hedingham.

Library of Congress Cataloging-in-Publication Data

Althea.
      Telling the truth / by Althea Braithwaite; photographs by
Charlie Best; illustrations by Conny Jude.
          p. cm. — (Exploring emotions)
      Includes bibliographical references and index.
      Summary: Examines the nature and importance of truth, explains
why telling the truth can sometimes be difficult, and describes the
negative effects of lying.
      ISBN 0-8368-2120-3 (lib. bdg.)
      1. Truthfulness and falsehood in children—Juvenile literature.
[1. Honesty.] I. Best, Charlie, ill. II. Jude, Conny, ill. III. Title.
IV. Series: Althea. Exploring emotions.
BF723.T8A57   1998
177'.3—dc21   98-5583

This North American edition first published in 1998 by
Gareth Stevens Publishing
1555 North RiverCenter Drive, Suite 201
Milwaukee, Wisconsin 53212 USA

This U.S. edition © 1998 by Gareth Stevens, Inc.
First published in 1997 by A & C Black (Publishers) Limited,
35 Bedford Row, London WC1R 4JH. Text © 1997 by Althea Braithwaite.
Photographs © 1997 by Charlie Best. Illustrations © 1997 by Conny Jude.
Additional end matter © 1998 by Gareth Stevens, Inc.

Series consultant: Dr. Dorothy Rowe

Gareth Stevens series editor: Dorothy L. Gibbs
Editorial assistant: Diane Laska

Printed in Mexico

1 2 3 4 5 6 7 8 9 02 01 00 99 98

Exploring Emotions

Telling the Truth

Althea

Photographs by
Charlie Best

Illustrations by
Conny Jude

18000

Gareth Stevens Publishing
MILWAUKEE

What does "telling the truth" mean?

When you tell someone something you know has happened or something you think or feel, you are telling the truth. When you say something happened, but it didn't, or say something you know is false, you are telling a lie.

Why do you think you should tell the truth?

If I tell a lie once, people won't believe me the next time.

I won't get in as much trouble as I will if I lie.
Lying makes me feel guilty.

Everyone tells lies at one time or another. Can you think of times when it's all right to tell a lie?

Ryan says, "Mom told a lie the other day. She told her friend I couldn't go to lunch with them because I already had plans that day. The truth was I don't get along with her children, so it's better if Mom goes alone with her friend.

I think that was a good lie; it didn't hurt anyone."

People sometimes tell small lies so they won't hurt other people's feelings. These lies are called "white lies" or "fibs."

Hannah was unhappy about her shoes. I didn't like them very much, but I told her they looked nice. She had to wear them to a party anyway, so why not make her feel better about them?

Sherri remembers, "When Mom bought a new dress and asked me if I liked it, I tried to avoid a lie by saying I liked the color. I didn't tell her the dress looked tight on her."

When Dad planned a surprise party for Mom, we had to lie a little so she wouldn't find out about it. We hid her presents, too.

Sometimes, telling the truth might ruin a surprise or give away a secret. If it's a good surprise that won't hurt anyone, it's usually all right to fib.

Tanice remembers, "When my brother asked me what Mom and Dad were giving him for his birthday, I lied and said I didn't know."

When it feels wrong to lie, you shouldn't do it. If someone asks you to keep a secret, but you don't think it's a good secret, you should tell the truth, even though it might get you, and maybe the other person, into trouble.

Nada says, "I feel very guilty when I tell a lie. Once, I got so sick Mom had to put me to bed. She couldn't understand what was wrong with me, and she was going to call the doctor, so I had to tell her about the lie. Now, every time I feel sick, she asks me lots of questions!"

11

Sometimes people will ask you to lie to keep them from getting into trouble.

Paul asked me not to tell when he stole candy from the store. It was too big a secret for me to keep, so I told my mom, and we talked about it.

Bullies can make you lie sometimes. They say they'll pick on you even more if you tell anyone what they're doing.

You might feel scared, but you have to try to be brave and tell the truth. Tell your parents, a teacher, or another adult you can trust. They should be able to help you with the situation.

13

People sometimes tell fibs to make themselves feel and sound more important. They might exaggerate or make up stories when they tell you what has happened to them.

Once, when we were talking about pets, Paul said he had a pet giraffe! Everyone laughed. Paul was always telling stories like that to try to make people notice him.

When everyone knows a story is not true, it's sometimes called a tall tale or make-believe.

I told everyone I had a candy bar in my lunch, when I only had a sandwich and an apple. I wanted to make them jealous.

This kind of lie is silly, because the things you have, or say you have, are not important. People like you for yourself, not for what you have.

People might like you less if you are always telling lies.

You might think telling a small lie will keep you out of trouble, but, sometimes, when you tell one lie, you have to tell another one to cover it up. You could end up in even bigger trouble. Can you think of a time when something like this happened to you?

Peter told his mom he had done his homework so he could watch TV. He lied — he hadn't studied his spelling words. The next day, he had to lie again. Peter told his teacher he had forgotten to take his spelling book home. The teacher called his mom, and Peter got into big trouble.

Mei says, "I copied my friend's math homework because I couldn't do the problems. Then the teacher gave us harder problems. I couldn't do them, so I had to tell her about copying my friend's work. She said I was foolish for cheating, because then she didn't know I needed help."

$6 \times 5 = 30$

When you tell the truth and people don't believe you, it feels very unfair.

"We were playing in the yard, and someone kicked the ball onto the roof of the shed. Everyone else ran away, so I got scolded, even though I didn't do it."

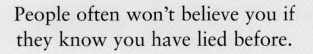

People often won't believe you if they know you have lied before.

Some adults accuse you of lying because they don't want what you told them to be the truth.

When I told Mom that my brother Raymond broke Mr. Kelsey's window, she said I was lying. I wasn't — I saw him do it.

Telling the truth can be very difficult when you know it is going to upset someone.

Tanice says, "I knocked a plate off the shelf, and it broke. I cleaned up the pieces and put them in the trash. I wanted to lie to Mom and say I didn't know anything about it, but, in the end, I was brave and told her. She was upset because she liked that plate, but I think she would have been more upset if I hadn't told her."

Ella remembers,
"When I was playing,
I broke a chair.
I felt sick because I
dreaded telling Mom.
She wasn't angry. She
said that these things
happen, and she was
glad I told the truth."

Sometimes you have
to be very brave to
tell the truth.

Some lies happen when adults forget what they have agreed.

If you clean your room now, we'll go to the movies later.

I cleaned my room. Can we go to the movies now?

Sorry, I'm busy. Maybe tomorrow.

Adults sometimes tell you lies because they think it is kinder to protect you from the truth. When something upsetting happens, adults often try to pretend nothing is wrong. Usually, you can tell something is wrong, and you start to worry about it.

It's much easier to understand and accept what's going on when people tell you the truth.

Mom was crying when I came in, so I knew Grandma must be very sick. Mom still kept telling me that Grandma was getting better.

People sometimes make you lie to yourself. When they tell you how you should or shouldn't feel, it can be hard to admit how you really feel.

Maria says she's not angry, even when she is. She's been told that good girls shouldn't get angry.

Sherri tries to tell herself she doesn't miss her dad, although she's very sad that she doesn't get to see him very much. She's been told that big girls don't cry.

It never helps to pretend that everything is all right when it's not. The only things you can ever know for certain are the things inside you — what you think and how you feel.

The most important person to be truthful with is yourself.

For Teachers and Parents
A Note from Dorothy Rowe

We all tell lies at one time or another, especially "little white lies" to avoid hurting someone's feelings. Even small lies, however, can hurt people because, when a lie is discovered, the trust between people is damaged, sometimes beyond repair. Teachers and parents know that the demands and consequences of telling the truth cause problems for children. Adults sometimes forget, however, that, in order to help, they first must find out how the child sees the problem.

A child won't see a situation the same way an adult does for the simple reason that, whatever their ages, no two people ever see things in exactly the same way. An adult shouldn't assume he or she knows what's wrong with a child but, rather, should explore possible reasons for the child's behavior by seeking answers to questions like: "Is this child lying because he or she is afraid of the consequences of telling the truth?" or "Is this child lying out of loyalty to a friend?"

Dozens of reasons are possible answers to the question, "Why does this child behave this way?" Thinking of these alternatives helps the adult ask better questions. The answers, however, can come only from the child.

Telling the truth is a challenge we face throughout our lives, and telling a lie, no matter how small, always means taking a risk. Adults must be prepared to share with children their own experiences, including the difficulties they have had telling the truth and the problems their lies have created. They should not pretend to provide easy solutions. This way, adults and children can explore the challenge of telling the truth together.

Suggestions for Discussion

To start a discussion and get everyone involved, have the children help you compile a list of specific situations that call for a choice between being truthful or lying. Then, with the children, decide for each situation whether telling the truth is "very important," "important," or whether it might be "all right to tell a lie."

Examples of situations in which people might be tempted to lie include:

- Saying you brushed your teeth, when you didn't.

- Eating the last piece of chocolate and pretending it wasn't you.

- Telling someone that you like his or her new haircut, when you think it looks terrible.

- Getting home late and saying it's because you had to stay at school, when you actually were playing at a friend's house.

Many issues dealing with truthfulness can be discussed with children while going through this book, page by page. The following points might help start your discussions.

Page 4
You want people to be honest with you. If everyone lied all the time, you wouldn't know who to trust.

Pages 6-7
We need to be very careful about telling even small lies. A white lie told to avoid hurting one person's feelings could end up hurting someone else, or the person you lied to might find out about it. Finding out that someone lied to you can sometimes hurt more than the truth.

Page 8
Think of and talk about other examples where telling the truth would mean spoiling a surprise or giving away a secret.

Page 9
Think of and talk about some examples where lying to keep a secret would feel wrong to you.

Page 11
Feeling guilty about lying might lead you to admit the truth, but that doesn't repair the trust broken by lying in the first place.

Page 13
Telling someone you are being bullied can be very difficult to do. Sometimes it helps to have a friend with you to give you courage and back you up.

Pages 14-15
When you have confidence in yourself, you don't need to make up stories to impress other people.

Page 17
Cheating on schoolwork or at games is the same as lying. It's usually very hard to regain the trust of someone who knows you have cheated at things in the past, and playing games with a person who cheats certainly is not much fun.

Pages 20-21
Accidents happen. When they do, people often get angry because they are upset about what was broken or damaged, rather than being angry at you for breaking it.

Page 23

Adults frequently tell children that something won't hurt them, even when they know it will; for example, a visit to the dentist. Perhaps, knowing what will happen, the adult is afraid to tell the child the truth. Telling the truth, however, gives the child a chance to prepare for the experience and might even make it more bearable. It's usually much easier to cope with something when you know the truth about it.

Pages 24-25

What about boys? Do good boys get angry? Do big boys cry?

A final point . . .

People see and remember things in different ways. When different people describe the same event, their versions might vary because each person is telling the truth as he or she remembers it. We all have preconceptions that color our interpretations of what happens and how something happens.

More Books to Read

Emotional Ups and Downs.
  Good Health Guides (series).
  Enid Fisher
  (Gareth Stevens)

If You Had to Choose, What Would
  You Do? Sandra M. Humphrey
  (Prometheus Books)

Keeping Secrets. Tormod Haugen
  (HarperCollins)

Liars. P. J. Peterson
  (Simon and Schuster)

Truth or Consequences. A. R. Plumb
  (Disney Press)

Videos to Watch

Cheating, Lying, and Stealing.
  (Film Ideas, Inc.)

Learning About Me.
  (Society for Visual Education, Inc.)

Name That Trouble.
  (Coronet/MTI Film & Video)

To Tell the Truth. (Churchill Media)

What Should You Do?
  Deciding What's Right.
  (Sunburst Communications)

White Lies. Live and Learn (series).
  (Beacon Films)

Web Sites to Visit

www.pbs.org/adventures/

KidsHealth.org/kid/feeling/

Due to the dynamic nature of the Internet, some web sites stay current longer than
others. To find additional web sites, use a reliable search engine with one or more
of the following keywords to help you locate information about telling the truth.
Keywords: *behavior, emotions, feelings, fibs, honesty, lies, trust, truth.*

Glossary

accept — to recognize information as true and be willing to understand or act on it to the best of your ability.

accuse — to charge someone with doing something wrong; to blame.

bully — a person who makes a habit of being mean or cruel to others, especially those who are weaker in some way.

cheating — breaking the rules; getting recognition or rewards in false or dishonest ways.

dread — extreme worry or fear about something coming up that is unpleasant or scary.

exaggerate — to make something sound bigger or better than it actually is.

false — not real, true, or correct.

fib — a lie about something unimportant or silly.

guilty — deserving blame for doing something wrong.

jealous — feeling hostile toward someone who you think has something that should rightfully be yours.

pick on — to give someone special, usually undesirable, attention; to tease or bully someone.

protect — to take care of; to guard from harm, loss, or injury.

told off — spoken to in a critical way; scolded harshly.

understand — to recognize, accept, and care about the circumstances of another person.

upset — feeling emotionally shaken up — especially hurt, worried, unhappy, troubled, or angry.

worry — to be concerned, disturbed, or fearful about something.

Index